CCSS **Genre** Expository Text

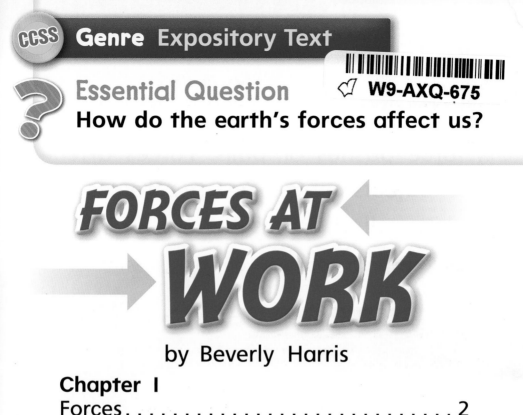

Essential Question
How do the earth's forces affect us?

W9-AXQ-675

FORCES AT WORK

by Beverly Harris

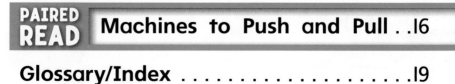

CHAPTER 1
FORCES

A force pushes or pulls. Forces affect how objects move. You see forces working all the time.

When you push someone on a swing, you use a force.

Pulling is a force, too.

A door swings open when you push it.

A grocery cart moves if you push it.

A door closes when you pull it shut.

A drawer opens if you pull it.

3

Gravity makes the baseball fall towards the ground.

Gravity is a force. It pulls objects. On Earth, gravity pulls objects toward the ground. Gravity even pulls you! You can test gravity. Drop a pencil. What happened? It fell. Why? Gravity pulled it down. It's true! Gravity works. You proved it.

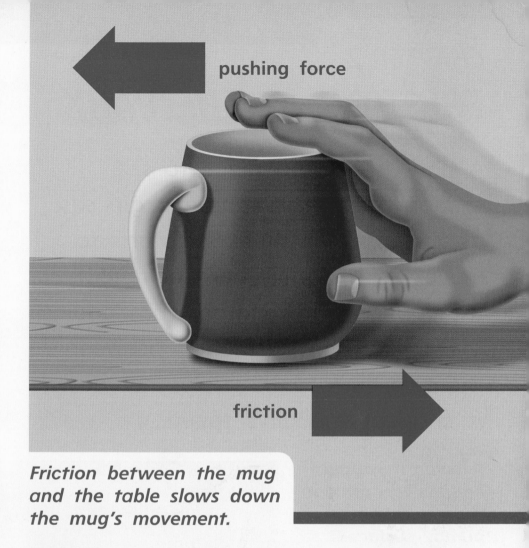

pushing force

friction

Friction between the mug and the table slows down the mug's movement.

Friction is another force. It affects how things move. It is different from gravity. Friction happens when two objects rub against each other. It slows down moving objects.

CHAPTER 2
FRICTION AT THE PARK

A park is a good place to see friction at work. Suppose a girl sits at the top of a slide. She starts to move. Gravity pulls her down. But the fabric of her clothes rubs against the slide. There is friction between the two **surfaces**. It slows her down. It changes the girl's speed.

A smooth surface creates less friction than a rough or bumpy surface.

The ball moves faster over short grass than long grass.

What if children play on the soccer field? They kick a ball. A kick is a push. It makes the ball move. As it moves, the ball rubs against the grass on the field. There is friction between the grass and the ball. It makes the ball slow down.

Friction also protects the children as they run. Their shoes rub against the ground. The friction keeps the children from slipping.

Cleats on soccer shoes create more friction between the ground and the shoe.

The player kicks the ball, pushing it up.

Suppose a soccer player kicks the ball in the air. Friction and gravity are both at work now. Gravity pulls the ball back toward the ground. Friction between the ball and the air slows the ball down a little bit.

CHAPTER 3
FRICTION AND STOPPING

A skater's movement also shows how friction works. Skates have smooth wheels. They roll easily on the path. There is friction where the wheels go over the path. Without the friction, the skater would slip and fall.

Friction between the ground and the skate helps a skater push off.

Friction helps a skater stop safely.

The skater makes more friction when trying to stop. The skater lifts the toe of the skate up, then puts the rubber stopper at the back down.

The stopper drags on the ground. Friction between the stopper and the path causes the skater to slow down. Then he or she comes to a stop.

Pushing with more force would make the bike move faster.

Forces work when a boy rides a bike. He pushes on the pedals. The pedals turn the wheels, and the bike moves.

When the boy wants to stop, he uses the brakes. This makes friction. The boy squeezes the brakes. The brakes grab the wheels. Then the pads rub against the wheels and cause friction. The bike's speed changes. The bike slows down and stops.

CHAPTER 4
LESS FRICTION

Sometimes we want things to make less friction. Think about a football. The ball has pointed ends. These help it go through the air without much friction. A player throws the ball. The ball zips through the air like a rocket.

A football's shape helps it move faster through the air than a round ball.

Swimmers at the 2008 Olympic Games wore special suits to make less friction.

At a swim meet, swimmers wear caps to cover their heads. They wear suits to cover their bodies. The caps and suits are slick and smooth. Now there is less friction between the swimmers and the water. The swimmers can swim fast like fish!

Forces are at work everywhere you look. What examples can you see?

Summarize

Use important details to help you summarize *Forces at Work.*

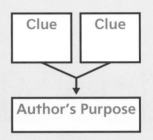

Text Evidence

1. How do you know *Forces at Work* is expository text? Genre

2. On page 5, is the author trying to entertain, inform, or persuade you? How can you tell? Author's Purpose

3. What is a football compared to on page 13? Use what you know about similes to help you. Similes

4. Write about the author's purpose for *Forces at Work.* Use selection details for support. Write About Reading

Compare Texts

How do machines help us push and pull?

Machines to Push and Pull

Gravity gives objects weight that we can measure. Heavy objects are hard to move. But machines can help us work against gravity. Amazing!

Force	Push	Pull
Moving a grocery cart	X	
Playing tug-of-war		X
Hitting a baseball	X	

Using a ramp helps these workers move a piano safely.

We can use machines as tools to help us push and pull heavy objects. Some machines are very simple.

Ramps

Some machines use inclined planes. An inclined plane is a flat surface that is raised on one end. A ramp is one example. It's easier to move a heavy object by sliding it up a ramp.

17

Levers

A lever is another kind of simple machine. A lever is a bar that rests on a support. The support is called a fulcrum. A force is **applied** at one end of the bar. This lifts the load at the other end. Levers help lift heavy things. A wheelbarrow is one kind of lever.

force

load

fulcrum

The man applies force when he pulls up on the handles of the wheelbarrow.

Make Connections

How does friction affect us?

Essential Question

What forces work when you use a wheelbarrow? Text to Text

Glossary

applied *(uh-PLIGHD)* brought into action; used *(page 18)*

friction *(FRIK-shuhn)* a force that happens when two things rub together *(page 5)*

gravity *(GRAV-i-tee)* a force that pulls things toward Earth and gives them weight *(page 4)*

surface *(SUR-fis)* the top or outside layer of something *(page 6)*

Index

Focus on Science

Purpose To show how friction works

What to Do

Step 1 You will need a toy car with wheels, a wooden block, and a measuring tape. Take your items to a room with no carpet.

Step 2 With a partner, take turns pushing the car and the block. Use the same force each time. Which item goes farther? Measure and record the distance.

Step 3 Repeat the activity in a carpeted room. What happens this time?

Conclusion Make a chart showing how far each item moved. Explain how the activity shows friction at work.